BANGE LERNHILFEN

Peter Luther
Jürgen Meyer

Englische Diktatstoffe
Unter- und Mittelstufe
Sekundarstufe I
Zur Festigung und Wiederholung von Rechtschreibung und Grammatik

C. Bange Verlag – Hollfeld

3. überarbeitete Auflage 1995

ISBN 3-8044-0647-5
© 1983 by C. Bange Verlag, 96142 Hollfeld
Alle Rechte vorbehalten!
Druck: Druckhaus Beyer GmbH, Langgasse 25, 96142 Hollfeld

Vorbemerkung

Die vorliegenden Diktatstoffe sind für die Unter- und Mittelstufe geeignet. Es wurde versucht, Themen und Texte zu berücksichtigen, die nach Länge, Inhalt und sprachlicher Schwierigkeit den Schülern dieser Spracherwerbsstufen angemessen sind. Gemäß den gestellten Anforderungen der recht unterschiedlichen Lehrplanrichtlinien wurden in einer Pointe gipfelnde, einfache sowie anpruchsvollere, kulturkundliche Texte gewählt. Da keine einheitlichen Richtwerte ermittelt werden konnten, wird man über die nach Länge und Schwierigkeitsgrad vorgenommene Einteilung streiten können. Es wird Aufgabe der Fachkolleginnen und -kollegen sein, ihre Wahl je nach dem Leistungsniveau ihrer Schüler zu treffen.

Im Unterschied zu den meisten auf dem Markt befindlichen Diktatsammlungen enthält das Bändchen eine kurze Einführung in die Bereiche der Groß- und Kleinschreibung und der Silbentrennung im Englischen.

Bei der unterrichtlichen Erprobung erwiesen sich zahlreiche Texte der Sammlung als durchaus geeignet für einen möglichen Einsatz in den Bereichen der Nacherzählungs- und Hörverstehensübungen. Selbst in Grundkursen der Gymnasialen Oberstufe konnte ein deutlicher Motivationsanstieg bei einer textlichen Bündelung zu dem Thema **British Humour** beobachtet werden. Übungsmöglichkeiten zur Festigung und Wiederholung grammatischer Erscheinungen bieten sich besonders an für die Schwerpunkte **Irregular Verbs, Sequence of Tenses** und **Reported Speech**. Die obigen Hinweise ergaben sich ebenfalls aus der Unterrichtspraxis.

Mögen sie von den Benutzern dieser Sammlung als Anregungen verstanden werden, die ihnen ihre tägliche Arbeit ein wenig erleichtern helfen sollen.

P. Luther   J. Meyer

Inhaltsverzeichnis

	Seite
Vorbemerkung	3
Große Anfangsbuchstaben	7
Die Trennung von Silben	8

Texte

Getting Nowhere	10
Not Everyboy's Darling	10
It Really Happened	10
A Lady Got Lost	11
On A Bus	11
They Are All Alike	12
A Monk's Hard Life	12
A Mother Reaction	12
Bad Luck	13
It Sounds Like Home	13
Convincing Performance	14
Young Ideas	14
Quick Money	15
An Admirable Housewife	15
Cultivated Taste	15
Calling On The Lord	16
English Breakfast	17
How Will You Know Unless I Tell You?	17
Einstein's Clever Chauffeur	18
The Klopman Diamond	18
Grandpa's Way Of Saving Energy	19
I Hate Mornings	20
The Spoken Word	20
Happy Birthday	21
Clever Animals	22
A Poor Country Family	22
Hard Times For Campers	23
Praise For English Cooking	25
Can Animals Think?	26
Ferrying Across The Channel	27
A Cunning Fraud	28
Holiday Switch To Save Fuel	28

Cocktail Party	29
Round The US In Seventy-eight Days	30
A Welcome Shock	31
Honesty	32
Collision	32
The Picture	33
Technically Impossible	34
The Stolen Fur	35
The Sales Manager	36
To Sweden As A Woodcutter	37
Malicious Dog For Sale	38
The North	40
Walking Again	41
The End Of The World	42
Sanctity Of Life	42
Pets	44
New Deal For The Commuters	44
Rescued	45
Poison Cloud	46
Video	47
British Motorists	48
Schools	49
Aerobics	50
Riding A Bike	51
Remember, Remember The Fifth Of November	52
Education	53
Dr. Anna Freud	53
25 Exciting Years	54
Health Problems In America	55
Does Your Dog Need A Diet Too?	56
Facts About The Freeze	57
A Winebook	58
Radiation	59

Die Wortzahlangaben befinden sich jeweils am Ende der Texte.

Große Anfangsbuchstaben

Im Englischen werden alle Wortarten kleingeschrieben. Dazu gehören auch die Substantive.
Großgeschrieben werden:
- das Personalpronomen 'I'
- Eigennamen von Personen: Peter, Mary, Jean, Uncle Robert, Aunt Carole
- Eigennamen von Ländern: Great Britain, France, Germany sowie die von ihnen abgeleiteten Adjektive: British, French, German
- Eigennamen von Flüssen: the Rhine, the Thames, Hudson River
- Eigennamen von Bergen: Snowdon, Mt. Everest
- Eigennamen von Straßen: Oxford Street, Green Street, the High Street
- Eigennamen von Gebäuden: Big Ben, the Tower, the Bank of England
- Wochentage, Monate, Feste: Monday, December, Easter
- Titel: Queen Mary, the Prince of Wales, King Henry, the Eighth, the Duke of Gloucester
- Substantiva aus dem religiös-politischen Bereich: the New Testament, the Lord, the Houses of Parliament, the Labour Party, the Liberals
- Schlußformeln in Briefen: Yours truly, With best wishes, All my love . . .
- das erste Wort in der direkten Rede: He asked the policeman, "Can you tell me the way to . . .?"
- Fachausdrücke: Indirect Object, Present Continuous
- das erste Wort am Satzanfang: Then he stopped reading.
- von Namen abgeleitete Adjektive: the British way of life, the Christian faith

Verbale Ableitungen von Eigennamen werden für gewöhnlich kleingeschrieben (to hoover, to shanghai), man findet sie aber auch mit Großbuchstaben (to Americanize). Ebenfalls kleingeschrieben werden Personennamen in allgemeiner Bedeutung (a foreign secretary) sowie Eigennamen, die zu Stoff- oder Gattungsnamen geworden sind (bolero, cardigan). Die Großschreibung von Wörtern in Buchtiteln, Schlagzeilen und Überschriften ist durch Regeln nicht eindeutig festgelegt. Für gewöhnlich werden Substantive, Adjektive und Zahlwörter groß-, Artikel und Präpositionen dagegen kleingeschrieben; oft entscheidet das Schriftbild über Groß- und Kleinschreibung.

Die Trennung von Silben.

Die Silbentrennung im Englischen ist sehr schwierig, so daß kaum einheitliche Regeln existieren. In vielen Lexika sind daher die Trennungsmöglichkeiten angegeben (z. B. in: **Dictionary of Contemporary English,** Langenscheidt-Longman).
Es wird abweichend vom Deutschen nach folgenden Grundregeln verfahren: Die Trennung erfolgt a) nach Sprach- und b) nach Sprechsilben.
zu a) Zusammengesetzte Wörter werden nach ihren Bestandteilen getrennt:
– when-ever, with-in, up-on, in-to, value-less, beauti-ful, in-side, after-noon, head-land, dust-bin.

Flexionsendungen sowie Vor- und Nachsilben werden vom Wortstamm abgetrennt:
– add-ing, box-ing, dress-es, loud-er, fast-est, mix-es, hunt-ed
– ab-negation, un-justified, pro-duction, re-nounce, co-operate, com-pare, con-ceive
– week-ly, king-dom, depend-ant, national-ism, butch-er, cook-er, sick-ness, fashion-able, govern-ment

Tritt Konsonantenverdoppelung ein, werden die Konsonanten getrennt:
– glad-der, cut-ting, snob-bish, snap-py, big-gest

Einsilbig gesprochene Wörter werden nicht getrennt:
– crook, might, crisp, dust, duke, due, spend, mist, run, moved

Stände bei der Trennung auf einer Zeile nur **ein** Vokal, wird nicht getrennt:
– **a**loud, **a**long, **a**lone, **e**dition, **e**nough, **i**deal

zu b) Die Trennung erfolgt wie im Deutschen:
- Treffen zwei Vokale aufeinander, werden sie getrennt: Janu-ary, the-atre
- Einzelne Konsonanten werden zur folgenden Silbe gezogen: so-cial, sa-lute, wa-ter
- Doppelkonsonanten werden getrennt: as-sociate, mut-ter, mut-ton
- Nach einem betonten, langen Vokal gehört ein einfacher Konsonant zur folgenden Silbe: au-tomat, dra-ma, au-tumn, trau-ma, fa-tal, fau-na
- Bei Ableitungssilben gehört ein einfacher Konsonant zur folgenden Silbe: offi-cial, ratifi-cation, over-due
- Nach einem betonten kurzen Vokal bleibt ein einfacher Konsonant bei der Silbe: en-ergetic, moth-er, lim-it, broth-er.

Beachte: –st– darf getrennt werden: regis-ter, mis-take, mis-ter.
In Zweifelsfällen sollte man die Silbentrennung überhaupt vermeiden!

Getting Nowhere

Spending our holidays in the Scottish Highlands, my husband and I went out for a drive one evening. We were soon hopelessly lost and could not find any road signs to guide us. Eventually, we saw a bus in the distance and thought that if we could get in front of it and see the destination, we would at least know in which direction we were heading.
At last, after following it several miles along the narrow lanes, we managed to pass it. Eagerly I turned round – only to read the words: "Mystery Tour."

ca. 100

Not Everybody's Darling

An old lady who often borrowed other people's drivers demanded to be driven away from a famous London hotel one day. Getting into the car, she asked the young man what his name was. "James," he said, only to be told she never addressed a driver by his Christian name.
"What's your surname?" she went on.
"Darling," came the answer.
She became red in the face and said: "Drive on, James."

ca. 75

It Really Happened

An English gentleman once invited the American reporter Stewart Alsop to his country house for the weekend. The writer was greeted at the door by the lady of the house, a grey-haired woman 'with a noble

face'. Beside her, Alsop told his listeners, was an enormous dog, which barked in markedly unfriendly fashion.
"Don't worry," said the lady, "Bobo never bites a gentleman." At which point, Bobo moved forward and planted his teeth in Alsop's right leg.

ca. 80

A Lady Got Lost

In a large ware-house a little girl helplessly wanders from one counter to the other, from one storey to the next. She begins to cry. Many people look at her and want to help her, but she doesn't answer to their kind questions. At last an aged shop-assistant succeeds in winning her confidence. „Please, says the little girl. Can't you help me. I have lost a lady with a little child. I am the little girl. I looked at the nice dolls and lost Mother. Grandmother says, I am as pretty as Mother is. So − if she is as pretty as I she is my mother. Did you see her?"

ca. 110

On A Bus

I could tell from the bus driver's greeting when a blind woman got on that she must be a daily passenger. She sat down directly behind him, and carried on a lively conversation as he drove.
When he reached the woman's stop, the driver got out and took her through heavy traffic to the other side of the street. As he returned to his seat, I saw the old woman still standing where he had left her. "She won't go until she knows I'm back safely," the bus driver explained to me. He blew the horn three times, and off we went.

ca. 100

They Are All Alike

When my first child was very small we lived in New York, where a favourite trip was to the Central Park Zoo. We always tried to get to the monkey house at feeding time. One day as I stood in front of the cages holding my son so that he could see better, I noticed standing next to me a woman holding in her arms a little boy about my son's age. We stood for some time in fascination watching the monkeys eating fruit and bread. Suddenly, at the same moment, each of us turned to the child in her arms and said, "Now you see, **he** eats the crust."

ca. 110

A Monk's Hard Life

Having decided to become a monk, a man joined an order where silence was the main rule. He could say only two words once every ten years.
After ten years the head monk called him in. "Well," he said, "you can say your two words now." The man replied, "Food cold," and left the office.
Another ten years passed, and this time the man said, "Bed hard."
After another ten years, the man was once again ordered into the head monk's office. "I'm leaving," he said. The head monk replied, "I'm not surprised. You've been complaining ever since you got here."

ca. 100

A Mother's Reaction

On a television show, in a discussion about embarrassing moments, Jack Ford, son of former President Gerald Ford, remembered a visit to the White House by the Queen.

"I was all excited and anxious to meet her," Ford remembered. "Hurrying to get into formal clothes, I could not find dress studs for my shirt and rushed to Dad's room to look for some.
Having no luck there, I ran down the corridor and pressed the lift button to return to my room. As the lift opened and I stepped in with my shirt unfastened, I found myself with the Queen, Prince Philip, and my mother and father. As Mother turned to introduce me, the Queen simply said, 'I have one just like that!'"

ca. 125

Bad Luck

After my husband and I spent a morning at the zoo with Joel, our four-year-old grandson, we stopped at a restaurant for lunch. My husband reached for his new glasses to read the menu and found that they were missing. "I know where they are, Grandpa," said our grandson.
"Where?" asked my husband, his face brightening.
"They're at the zoo," Joel replied. "When you took me off the train by the elephants, they fell out of your pocket." Trying to control his anger, my husband asked, "Joel, if you saw my glasses fall out, why didn't you tell me?"
"Well, Grandpa," explained Joel, "after you stepped on them, I didn't think you wanted them any more."

ca. 120

It Sounds Like Home

A woman was busy cleaning when the telephone rang. Going to answer it, she fell over a floor mat and, grabbing for something to hold on to, seized the telephone table. It fell over with a crash, the receiver falling onto the floor. As it fell, it hit the family dog, who leaped up, howling. The woman's three-year-old son, surprised by this noise, broke into loud screams.

The woman said some unfriendly word. She finally managed to pick up the receiver and lift it to her ear, just in time to hear her husband's voice on the other end say, "Nobody's said hello yet, but I'm sure I have the right number."

ca. 120

Convincing Performance

On a visit to New York, we discovered a computer which, for one dollar, accepts your signature on a small card, and in return gives a computer analysis of your personality.

We all had a go at it and, with the exception of my brother-in-law, were satisfied with the reports handed out. He is an engineer and challenged the correctness of the machine by making the same signature on another card and feeding it to the computer. A few strange sounds and back came the card with a report like the first one, but with an additional piece of advice: "Try to be more trustful."

ca. 100

Young Ideas

Friends tell how their sixteen-year-old daughter came home late one night from a party with a crowd of youngsters. They burst into the house, turned on the record player, and made a lot of noise in the kitchen preparing a snack. When her friends finally made their last noisy goodbyes, the girl switched off the record player, turned out the lights, went into her parents' room and whispered, "I'm home."

ca. 70

Quick Money

A doctor who sometimes drank a good deal at dinner was called one evening to a patient. Feeling her pulse and finding himself unable to count it, he said in a low voice, "Drunk, by God!" Next morning, feeling troubled, he was wondering what explanation of his behaviour he could offer when he received a letter from her.
She knew only too well, wrote the patient, that he had discovered the cause of her illness. But she begged him to keep it secret in consideration of the enclosed – a cheque for £50.

ca. 100

An Admirable Housewife

My neighbour on the next farm was the best organized housewife I've ever met. She made her children's clothes, baked all the family's bread, worked in the fields in busy seasons and looked after an enormous garden. As her family grew older, she played the church organ for weddings and funerals and also acted as a teacher.
One evening I called in to find her just back from the shops, her hungry family about to come in from the fields for supper. She quickly put a frying-pan on the stove and cut an onion into it. A marvellous smell soon filled the kitchen.
"That's something I learned as a bride," she said, laughing. "Even if supper is two hours away they'll go happily about their work, knowing that something's cooking."

ca. 130

Cultivated Taste

James Buchanan, one of the first distillers to make blended Scotch whisky popular in London, also had a nice line in humour. Faced with a

London hotel which had so far refused to stock Buchanan's Blend, so the story goes, he hired a dozen handsome unemployed actors to join him at a specially ordered dinner there. They sat down and the wine waiter approached. "What will you start with, sir?" he asked the attractive young man who had been placed at the head of the table.
"Buchanan Blend," was the reply.
An uncomfortable silence followed. "I'm sorry. We don't have that, sir."
"What! No Buchanan?" screamed the company in well-drilled horror. "We can't dine here." And they went out, under the fascinated look of their fellow diners.

ca. 130

Calling On The Lord

Once every three minutes, every day of the year, it is believed that someone somewhere in England picks up a telephone and dials one of the country's successful church telephone centres run by priests and trained members of all religions, who act as helpers in all problems.
The telephone churches first offer callers a recorded prayer, encouraging religious words, or a sermon. Most of these are changed daily, rarely run for more than three minutes and end with an invitation to call another number if further help is needed.
It is a form of direct religious fellowship which is meeting a widespread need, with some 200,000 calls recorded every year. Some callers are disillusioned with traditional religion, but most helpers say that 'empty-heartedness', a desire for a purpose in life, is the common cause.

ca. 140

English Breakfast

British people are eating fewer breakfasts, according to a survey of 6,000 homes by the Kellogg Company of Great Britain. In 1956 half the population had a cooked breakfast; last year the amount fell to a fifth. And quite a lot of people, including 500 000 children, had nothing to eat at all. The company believes that the fall of the cooked breakfast is the result of the rise in the number of working mothers. Some children now go hungry for 18 hours between tea at home at about 6.30 p.m. and lunch at school the next day.
Says Professor Arnold Bender of Queen Elizabeth College, London: "Teachers have reported that hungry children are without interest, nervous, careless, and are unable to concentrate."

ca. 125

How Will You Know Unless I Tell You?

Cold rain lashed across the window, lowering my spirits, already suffering from my long illness. Get-well cards had stopped coming. A faded plant, a gift from fellow teachers, was all that remained of the flowers I had received. I felt lonely, unimportant, forgotten by a world that obviously was doing very well without me.
Then the post arrived, bringing a note from a teacher I passed each morning on my way to school. "Dear Jane," she said. "My class is about to begin, but I must write these few words before my pupils arrive. I missed your smile this morning, just as I have every day since you've been ill. I hope you'll be well soon. You're probably surprised at receiving this note, but the world for me is a less happy place without you. And how will you know unless I tell you?"
Suddenly, my despair slipped away. Someone missed me; someone needed me. That message worked better than any medicine the doctor could give me.

I reread the words carefully. The last sentence held my attention: "How will you know unless I tell you?" I wouldn't have known, of course, and I would still have been lonely and sad. How can any of us know what's in the minds and hearts of others – unless we receive some word, some gesture?

ca. 230

Einstein's Clever Chauffeur

There's a story about how Albert Einstein was travelling to universities in a chauffeur-driven car, making lectures on his theory of relativity. During one journey, the chauffeur remarked: "Dr. Einstein, I've heard you make that lecture about 30 times. I know it by heart and I bet I could give it myself."
"Well, I'll give you the chance," said Einstein. "They don't know me at the next college, so when we get there I'll put on your cap, and you'll introduce yourself as me and give the lecture."
The chauffeur gave Einstein's lecture perfectly. When he had finished, he started to leave, but one of the professors stopped him and asked a difficult question filled with mathematical problems. The chauffeur thought fast. "The solution to that problem is so simple," he said, "I'm surprised you have to ask me. In fact, to show you just **how** simple it is, I'm going to ask my chauffeur to come up here and answer your question."

ca. 160

The Klopman Diamond

The airliner had just taken off and all the passengers had settled down. In the first-class section, a man sat next to a well-dressed woman who was wearing an attractive diamond chain.

"Excuse me, but I couldn't help noticing that beautiful necklace," he said. "It's the most perfect stone I've ever seen."
"Why, thank you," she said, "It's the Klopman diamond, you know."
He looked puzzled, "I'm sorry, but I don't think I have ever heard of it."
"Well, it's a lot like the Hope diamond. It's not as large, of course, but the beauty of the Klopman is the same. And, just like the Hope diamond, it comes with a curse for the person wearing it."
"That's really amazing! What kind of curse?"
"Mr Klopman."

ca. 130

Grandpa's Way Of Saving Energy

Grandpa would have been in his element these days. Not that he knew much about saving energy – saving money was Grandpa's theme.
Our heating was never turned on until late November. "Not cold enough for the heating yet," he would say, rubbing his hands. "It's not going on until we need it."
It was the same with electric light. It had to be dark enough not to see before Grandpa allowed the lights – or rather the light – on. To leave a light on if nobody was in the room really annoyed him. "You're wasting kilowatts," he would shout. Every few days he would go and look at the metre.
The way Grandpa went on about the fridge, we were lucky to eat. "Every time that door is opened," he'd say, "you're wasting electricity. When you open the door you're letting the cold out and it has to run to get cold again." His closed-door policy may not have saved the environment but it saved money.
Petrol? Well, we didn't have a car so we did use none – a 100-per-cent saving. And the way Grandpa worked out distance, public transport was a sort of necessary evil. "You're not going to catch a bus," I can hear him say. "Why, boy, you're only going two miles."
Maybe he had something there.

ca. 225

I Hate Mornings

It is Friday morning when I am writing this, and it is, I think, a beautiful morning. I have been up for several hours already and I have managed quite a bit, and now there is something I very much want to do. I want to go back to bed.
I am trying to be a morning person. I have been trying now for some time, getting up early, eating a proper breakfast, having a shower, dressing, reading the papers – trying, in short, to be awake. I am not.
I am not a morning person. It is not my fault. It is a handicap like being short or left-handed when you're young and want to look tough. I am expected to work when others work, to come out of the house with a smile on my face, kicking my heels the way they do in the television commercials – to greet the morning with a smile. It is useless. It is unfair.
I know doctors are going to have their ideas about all this – how maybe I'm afraid to face life or such things. I tell you this is not the case. I love life. It's the morning I hate.
ca. 200

The Spoken Word

There is a powerful social argument for establishing a standard of spoken English – allowing for regional variations and the individual's own occasional differences. Nothing divides the classes more in Britain than the way they speak. Do away with the independent schools, offer university education to everybody, reduce the financially upper classes by taxes, give equal rights to everybody by governmental means, and Britain will remain in separate levels as it is now by accents and pronunciation – unless the ladder of equal opportunity open to all leads to the use of a common spoken tongue.
Good grammar and clear expression, everyone agrees, must be taught and must be learnt. There is no reason why the same should not apply to good pronunciation. If it were so, Britain would be on the way to

becoming a nation which would understand itself better.

ca. 145

Happy Birthday

The laws set up certain standards concerning age – you can get married at 16, drive a car at 17, buy alcohol at 18. These are helpful and even necessary rules to have. But we need to set minimum ages for a wider range of activities. Too many people are confused if they are old enough to do what they want to do.
What is the minimum age at which you can refuse invitations by saying, "I don't want to go"? The generally accepted answer is 70. You may find that it is perfectly correct to turn down things you don't want to do as early as 55. On the other hand, certain conservative people insist that you have to keep finding excuses for not going somewhere until you are 85 or dead, whichever happens first.
At what age is it proper to give up your job? 65. What is the minimum age at which funny birthday cards cease to be funny? 59. What is the minimum age for learning to ski? There is no minimum age. There is, however, a maximum age, which is three.
Some things can't be too accurately fixed.
When are you old enough to sit down at a party when everybody else is standing up and complaining that their feet, legs or backs are killing them? 47. I say 47 because it was at this age that I first sat down and discovered you could get away with it.
At what age are men most attractive to women? Four years ago.
At what age is it considered proper to begin complaining about the dreadful young people today? It used to be that you weren't supposed to complain about the young until you were over 30. Now you find some people of 17 asking when kids of 18 are going to show some signs of maturity.
We need to fix our rules in these matters. Otherwise we will have complete chaos, for which our society has long passed the minimum age.

ca. 340

Clever Animals

Joe Miller travelled a lot around the country. He was a commercial traveller. He spent the nights almost only in hotels, in nice ones, and not so nice ones, but mostly in not so nice ones.

One day his business took him to Blackstone. Joe Miller had not been to the little town before, he was there for the first time. There were only two hotels. Joe looked at them carefully. Then he decided on the 'Carlton'. The receptionist greeted him with a bow. "I'd like a room," Joe demanded. "Very well, sir," said the receptionist and bowed his head. "Yes, sir, if you would be so kind as to put your name in the guestbook. You can have No. 14." Joe nodded and carefully wrote his name under a long row of others. Then he looked once again at what he had written. Suddenly his eyes opened wide: A large bug was slowly crawling over the paper! The receptionist hurried up to him: "Is anything wrong?" Joe silently pointed to the insect: "I have seen a lot in my time. Not only are there bugs here, but I have never experienced them looking through the guestbook to see which room number one has."

ca. 200

A Poor Country Family

While driving through France during the last war, writer W. Somerset Maugham, late at night without a place to stay, was invited by his driver to spend the night with some cousins of hers. She didn't name them and said rather shyly, "They're very simple people." Maugham, expecting a poor country family, describes what happened:

We were received by a short, fat man with a red face. He looked the typical Frenchman.

"Did you find a bottle of brandy in your room?" he asked me.

"I didn't look," I said.

"I always keep a bottle of brandy in every bedroom in the house, even

the children's rooms. They never touch it, but I like to know it's there."
I thought this was strange, but I said nothing. We went in to dinner and found waiting for us two girls of perhaps 14 and 15 with their governess. We were waited on by an old butler and a maid. My host said, "I've opened my last bottle of excellent red wine for you." I had never seen such a big bottle before, and I was impressed. It was delicious. For a poor cousin I thought my host was doing very well. The food was excellent, too. One dish was so good that I was forced to remark on it. "I'm glad you liked that," said my host. "Everything in this house is cooked in brandy." I began to think it was a very strange house indeed, and I wished I knew who on earth this generous person was. We finished dinner and had some coffee. Then the butler brought some glasses and a large bottle of brandy. I thought it wise not to take any more alcohol, so when it was offered to me I refused. "What," cried my host, "have you come to spend the night in the house of Martell and you refuse a glass of brandy?"
I had been dining in the house of the most famous brandy merchant in the world.

ca. 340

Hard Times For Campers

A few years ago the search for the sun led to a rush of holidaymakers to the South of France, where hotels and inns were fully booked and camping sites overcrowded. In some places, 280,000 campers were competing for space sufficient for only 165,000. The local officials allowed an overload of 130 per cent on camping sites. Tents were pitched, only inches apart. The coastal area suffered from permanent traffic jams and was polluted by fumes. People resorted even more than in the past to wild camping pitching their tents or parking their caravans wherever there was space. The concentration of campers in certain areas led to quarrels. Some of the local people took the side of the campers because they felt it good for the trade in the area. Others came out against them, in the name of protection of the environment and public health. The Dutch and the Germans were considered a special target for criticism. Local people even nicknamed them the 'invaders'! Hostilities broke out here and there, with blows and some serious injuries, but when the first rain came, the opponents cooled down and decided to live in peace.

ca. 200

Praise For English Cooking

England's cooking has never been held in high esteem because of its tastelessness and simplicity. Now however, this opinion has radically changed. In his recently published 'Good Food Guide' Christopher Driver has maintained that England's cooking is better than its reputation and that it can be favourably compared with France's cuisine. In his book he examines numerous restaurants in Great Britain. The proprietors of the top restaurants in the big cities, mainly in London, were looking forward to the book. But in his preface, Driver criticizes these proprietors in particular because of their arrogance and their self-satisfaction. Most of the praise for English cooking did not go to them, but to the many small restaurants run by amateurs and foreigners who cook very tasty dishes. These foreign cheap-restaurants are on the increase and are becoming more and more popular with all the customers. Christopher Driver has been testing restaurants anonymously for many years and his ratings in the 'Good Food Guide' met with a lot of approval and brought about various improvements. Therefore, Continental tourists should not trust the old prejudice against English cooking, but should go to England and form their own opinion. It will certainly be worthwhile!

ca. 200

Can Animals Think?

Jokes have often been made about the thinking capability of animals and the dear creatures were never offended. They have more of a sense of humour than people. For example, people maintain that carp swim under a bridge when it is raining as they do not want to become wet! In the same way it is joked that May bugs stop flying around on the first of June. The story about the circus elephant is also told: During the performance he seized an old acquaintance sitting in the third row. The elephant had got a piece of sugar many years ago from that old friend. Therefore he stretched out his trunk, quickly picked up the friendly gentleman and placed him in one of the best seats. There are other stories to the same effect. The following episode was actually seen: Squirrels placed very hard nuts on the surface of a road so that passing cars could attend to the cracking. This method was generally successful and if you had observed the squirrels afterwards at their banquet, then it is easy to see why they are called 'The monkeys of the forest'. Nowadays, dogs who wait at the traffic lights showing red until the colour green lights up allowing them to cross are no rarities in the cities. Capability to think? Ability to combine observations? Instinct? Who knows what it is.

ca. 230

Ferrying Across The Channel

Whether you are on the Continent and planning a holiday in England or in England and considering a Continental holiday, the English Channel is no barrier to your plans. It is easy, economical and fun to ferry across.

During peak travel periods, a lot of companies offer numerous crossings a day to and from England. Each of the several routes across the Channel is linked to fast motorways both on the Continent and in Britain. All ships offer a simple drive-on, drive-off loading and unloading system.

A lot of short-holiday cross-Channel bargain tickets are offered every year, reductions are also available to motorcyclists, bicycles get a free ride and foot passengers receive bargain rates. On-board facilities include restaurants, cafeterias, bars, duty-free gift shops and banks for currency exchange. Cabins are available and are particularly comfortable for night crossings. Some of the ships even have dance floors and film showings. For a relaxing start to a holiday or a quiet day after a busy holiday, people's most favourite room aboard ship is the "quiet room". This room has special seats and is indeed quiet. You can read, snooze or open the curtain and watch the sea. You are free to stroll on deck, but you must get everything out of your car that is necessary because you will not be allowed to return to it during the crossing. This is both for your own and your car's safety. On arriving in England travellers can take advantage of the recently opened Dover Motel, conveniently located on the A2 London Road and for those visiting the Continental coast, cheap accommodation is available at many seaside resorts including camping and caravan parks.

ca. 280

A Cunning Fraud

Henry ambled through the town after a boring day in the office. The free evening did him good after a day with unpleasant bosses, stupid secretaries and a mountain of uninteresting files. Henry sighed and quickened his pace. He was looking forward to a visit to his local pub, where some friends were waiting for him.
"Evening Post! Cunning swindler in our town! Twelve people his victims! Evening Post!" the newspaper boy's loud voice interrupted Henry's happy thoughts. Henry pondered: "Cunning swindler in our town? I must buy the paper. We'll have something to talk about in the pub." He called the boy over, pulled out some change and bought a paper. Henry's eyes flew over the headlines on the first page. He could not see anything about a swindler and turned over the next page. There was not anything there either. Henry turned to the third page and kept on turning. One sensation after another, but not a single line about the fraud so loudly proclaimed by the newspaper boy. Strange, quite strange, Henry thought and looked for the boy. He could just see him disappearing around the next corner. He could hear his voice, too: "Evening Post! Cunning swindler in our town! Already thirteen people his victims! Evening Post!"

ca. 210

Holiday Switch To Save Fuel

A cut in the six-week summer holiday for schools and the extension of the Christmas and Easter breaks is being proposed by the Inner London Education Authority to save energy.
The Labour-controlled authority spends £ 13,500,000 a year on heating and lighting schools and colleges. It has estimated that £ 35,000 could be saved for every day they are closed during mid-winter.

A confidential memorandum has been sent to the heads of all 1,200 schools controlled by the authority – the biggest education body in the country – warning them that the energy crisis is likely to worsen next winter. It urges them to review the 'pattern of school holidays' with their staffs for next year and report to their boards of governors in the autumn. Plans by some primary schools to lengthen the Whitsun half-term holiday are to be scrapped.
At present, schoolchildren receive 83 days holiday a year – 42 days are taken during the summer, 17 days at Christmas and 18 days at Easter. Three half-term days and May Day and occasional days make up the remainder.
The proposal is almost certain to anger both parents and teachers, whose main family holidays are invariably planned for the summer months.

ca. 200

Cocktail Party

If someone has to invite a lot of people and has very little room to seat them, then he gives a cocktail party. Host and hostess are at the entrance of the house and welcome their guests, who are then served drinks and sandwiches by the servants and then stand around forlorn, left alone with their fate.
One of those people left to their own devices at such a cocktail party was a young man who came breezing in, kissed the hostess' hand, shook hands with the host, snatched a Martini, grabbed a few sandwiches and stood in a corner.
"Aren't these drinks purest dishwater!" he remarked to the young lady who was standing beside him. He understood the movement of her head as approval. "And how poor these sandwiches are! I would have brought some from home, if I had known." She looked at him

sympathetically. "Just look at the lady of the house!" he continued, "she could really have gone to the hairdresser's before the party, let alone our host's creased tie." – "By the way, do you know who I am?" the young lady smiled. "No, unfortunately not." – "I am the daugther." For a moment he was speechless. "Do you know who I am?" he asked at last. "No," she said. "Thank goodness!" he sighed and disappeared.

ca. 210

Round The US In Seventy-eight Days

Recently, sixty-year-old Jean Williams from Illinois completed in New York a seventy-eight-day motorbike trip across the United States. Her dream had always been to cross the United States by motorbike, but her profession and lack of money had prevented it. Finally however, she had saved enough money and interrupted her job. She had thought her trip would take eighty days, when she set off from New York at the beginning of April. Her trip was supposed to cover a distance of 20,000 kilometres. She travelled through the East of the United States, crossed the Mississippi at St. Louis and travelled through the Midwest in sunshine and rain without any unusual occurrences.

Jean had only two minor breakdowns and had to clean the spark plugs several times, something which she had practised beforehand. After all, she is the secretary of the American Motorcycle Club! On route she visited a lot of friends who always welcomed her with open arms and admired her daring and enterprising spirit. In the middle of May, Jean arrived at San Francisco and was given a hearty reception. After a short stay she returned via the Southern States and reached New York again in mid-June.

On the trip she got to know her country well and at the end she declared that it had been wonderful. She beamed with satisfaction when she was welcomed by the Governor of New York.

Jean Williams, a mother of six children and grandmother of ten, began to ride a motorbike eleven years ago and at the beginning explored her near surroundings on many trips. Then she joined the American Motorcycle Club, became its secretary and since then has ridden 160,000 kilometres on her motorbike. In the meantime, she has had four different motorbikes and has the reputation of being a very careful rider: Up to now she has never had an accident! We wish her all the best for her future trips!

ca. 325

A Welcome Shock

It happened five days before Christmas, when the Jones family were having supper. There was a terrible storm that night. Suddenly the chimney collapsed and crashed through the roof of the Jones' house in Winchester Lane in the English town of Bradford. Grandma Jones was so shocked and horrified that she jumped up and started swearing. Normally, it is not the done thing for old ladies to swear, but on this occasion her swearing was heartily welcome by the whole family – the nicest Christmas present they could think of! Five years ago Grandma Jones had suffered a stroke and since then had to spend her life in a wheelchair. Her left side was paralyzed and after the stroke she hadn't been able to speak at all. Later she made herself understood by whispering. The collapse of the chimney was a terrible shock for her, when the ceiling came down, she was sitting in her wheelchair.
Fortunately, the family is well insured so that they do not have to pay for the damage. The only disadvantage is that they will have to spend Christmas in rather a cold house!

ca. 200

Honesty

When John Smith got into the bus, a young man greeted him: "Good morning, Mr Smith," he said, "here is the twenty pence you lent me yesterday." – "This must be a mistake," John replied, "I didn't lend you anything." – "But of course," the other man insisted, "you were standing on the platform near a tall, dark-haired man. When I got into the bus at Frisco Street and wanted to pay, I only had a pound note on me. The conductor could not change it. Then you paid my fare for me." John was surprised. He was nervous. Who is not nervous nowadays? Up to now, he had not experienced such a case of complete loss of memory. What the young man told him, was as completely unknown to him as the language of the Eskimos! "Please, take the money!" the other one requested, "it must be settled."
A fortnight later, John was addressed by the young man again: "Excuse me, Mr Smith, please, don't think me impertinent, when I have to bother you again with a favour. I really must catch the eight o'clock train to Glasgow and have just realized that I have forgotten my wallet. Could you lend me £ 5 until tomorrow? You'll get it back – cross my heart!" John stopped and put his hand in his pocket. If a man who even pays his non-existing debts is not honest, who is honest?
He neither saw the polite man again nor his money.

ca. 250

Collision

John Carpenter became very worried when his wife was not home at 6 p. m. after her maiden trip in his new car. In his mind he already saw his beautiful car being towed by some enormous break-down lorry. Confusing sums of money resulting from such an enterprise whirled in his head. He should not have allowed her to take the car. After all, she had only passed her driving test yesterday. How could he have been so mad – his beautiful new car! His pessimistic thoughts were interrupted by the sound of his wife putting the key in the lock to open the door. He pounced on her and asked breathlessly: "What's happened, Hilda? Where on earth have you been?" – "Oh, I met Mary," she said and dropped into an armchair, exhausted. He was unbelievably relieved. The fact that she had met Mary explained everything. Mary had her own car and the two friends had probably had a chat about horsepower and driving comfort. He felt so happy that he immediately mixed her a cocktail and brought her her slippers. Afterwards he sat at her feet cross-legged and asked: "Where did you meet, Mary?" Hilda's voice was no more than a whisper: "On our left mudguard, darling. But the mechanic at the garage promised to have the car repaired in a fortnight."

ca. 220

The Picture

John saw a picture in an art dealer's shop-window which immediately fascinated him. Suddenly an idea occurred to him: In a week's time it was his first wedding anniversary. He wanted to give Maureen the picture as a present. She would be thrilled. Without hesitating he bought it. "I only have £ 5 on me," he said to the sales assistant, "but I'll come back tomorrow and pay the rest." The next day the boss himself was in the shop. "I'm sorry," he said to John, "but I had already sold the picture the day before yesterday. Unfortunately, I forgot to tell my sales assistant." John could not hide his disappointment. "I'll give your buyer £ 5 more for it." – "Our buyer is a young lady," answered the dealer, "I do not know whether she will agree with your suggestion." – "She has to," said John, "I have the same right she has. I bought the picture as well." The dealer became uneasy. There were many other pictures of the same value and charm. John only had to choose, but he insisted on his demand. Finally the dealer asked him to wait a while. Probably the lady would come in again in the next day or two. After three days John paid his third visit to she shop. "The lady was here an hour ago," complained the dealer, "but she does not want to sell." They talked again for a while, but came to no decision. "Here is the address of the young lady, pay her a visit, talk to her, marry her! Then all quarrelling is unnecessary and superfluous." John crumpled the little piece of paper together, but fascination and longing grew. The picture pursued him by day and by night. He wanted it, he had to have it. Whether he liked it or not, he had to pay a visit to the hard-hearted lady. He found the piece of paper in his coat pocket, smoothed it out and – read Maureen's address.

ca. 320

Technically Impossible

The young poet had recited his own works for the first time. Of course, not on the stage of an important cultural town, but quite modestly in his own home town. The audience had listened and even clapped here and there, firstly, because it was the done thing, secondly, because they had had free tickets and thirdly, because the poet's father was an important and esteemed citizen. Who was to decide whether his poetry was good or bad? That is very difficult to define with modern lyrics, and the lyrics which the young poet had offered were very up to date. Anyway, it was a success and it had to be celebrated, privately of course, and together with the followers of the ambitious genius. Glasses were raised, many a compliment was to be heard, and the young poet revelled in the joy of his first success.
Something, however, gave him cause for thought. The reporter of the local paper, who was also there, enjoyed the good wine, but otherwise

he did not say anything. After all, what he said mattered. The young poet was too eager to be able to wait for the next edition of the paper. Thus, he asked the critic for his opinion. The journalist looked silently into his glass. "Neither Keats nor Wordsworth could have written some of your poems," he said finally. The poet blushed with pride. "Do you really mean that?" – "Of course, I do," the reporter confirmed. "And which poem do you mean?" The critic answered: "The one about the telephone and the one about television."

ca. 270

The Stolen Fur

Harry cuddled up in his fur coat. He was leaving the tearoom. He hurried home because the snow was falling heavily and the wind was whistling through the empty streets. A fur coat like this is worth its weight in gold, mumbled Harry to himself stroking the warm, expensive coat. The streets became darker as the lonely wanderer approached his house. The darkness was absolutely impenetrable and even the white snow did not help. The street lamps hardly gave any light that night. Only a few yards and I'll be home, Harry thought. Thank goodness!
Suddenly a figure came up to him and a torch was thrust into his face. The stranger scrutinized the pedestrian in his fur coat and said in a demanding voice: "Take off the fur coat!" Harry was frightened. "Come on," said the man. A pistol gleamed in the light of the torch. "Take off the coat!" he said once more, "Hurry up, I do not have much time!" Harry wanted to gain time. "Look, sir . . ." – "I have no time to look. Come on, take it off!" Harry had to hand over the valuable coat. The man put his thin, patched coat around him and took the elegant fur coat for himself. "Marvellous," mumbled the robber, "Oh, that's much better. Thank you, sir! Beaver inside, opossum outside. Fine." – Harry

shivered in the shabby coat. The robber wanted to run away, when Harry whispered, shivering: "One moment, please! I'd like to ask you something." – "Yes, what's the matter?" – "What are you going to do now?" The robber laughed self-satisfied: "I am going to drink a hot cup of tea in Lyon's Tea Shop." – "I wouldn't advise you to do that." – "Why not?" "Because the owner of the fur coat is also sitting there drinking tea."

ca. 300

The Sales Manager

"A marvellous chap!" – "A sales genius!" – "We'll have to look at him!" – "Let's have a look at him!" Then the two managing directors of the giant department store drove over to Bentville to look at the new branch manager there, who increased his sales every month.
They found him talking to a customer. "This rod, sir?" asked the branch manager in a friendly way. "It is extremely expensive." – "But it is the best you can get, sir. It is certainly worth thirty dollars." – "But there are also rods for three dollars, aren't there?" – "Of course, sir, but that is not good enough for you." – "Alright, I'll take this rod." The sales manager bent forward confidentially: "Where are you going fishing, sir, if I might ask?" – "I thought of Yellowstone Park," the customer said slowly. The branch manager shook his head: "That poor lake? I know of a lake full of fish – trout and salmon, hidden away in the Rockies, only, only . . . the lake is completely cut off. You have a caravan?" – "Unfortunately not," confessed the customer. "Never mind, we have marvellous caravans in stock."
One hour later the customer had bought a car, a tent, a radio, an airmattress, a stove, because there were no hotels on the lake.
The customer had hardly left she shop, when the two managing

directors ran up to the branch manager. "A marvellous sales achievement! To sell a man who only wants a fishing-rod for three dollars goods the value of $ 5,000!" The branch manager said smilingly: "Who said anything of a fishing-rod? The man came into the shop and demanded a packet of handkerchiefs for his wife. I asked him whether his wife had a cold. "If you stay at home, you'll only have worry. Why don't you go fishing during that time?"

ca. 310

To Sweden As A Woodcutter

I saw him sitting on the bank of the river. He was counting his money. He was a boy of about ten. I sat down beside him. "You are rich, aren't you?" I said. He looked at me disapprovingly. As I did not look too grown-up, he plucked up courage and asked me a question: "Do you know how much it costs to go to Sweden?" – "What on earth do you want in Sweden?" – "I want to be a woodcutter." – "You have picked on a difficult job. What makes you want to be a woodcutter?" – "Sweden is a beautiful country and I like forests. Cutting trees is not as difficult as school. At home and in school they all expect too much of me and I don't get on with my classmates either." – "Do you want to go to Sweden on your own?" – He didn't reply to my question. He was a little boy full of dreams. "You won't manage it today anyway. It's getting dark. You first have to go by train and then by boat," I said. His little face put on a helpless look. "What do you think of the idea of me coming with you to Sweden?" He looked at me doubtfully. After a while he said: "Alright, then". I suggested, "We spend the night on the river bank and leave at the crack of dawn". We settled down. It was warm. Within two hours I knew all his troubles. I gave him some advice as to how to get on with his classmates and promised to help with his homework. His pensive eyes lit up a little: "But what about our trip to Sweden?" he asked. A cold wind blew over from the river, he shivered and yawned. "Perhaps we can postpone our trip for a little while," I said carefully. He agreed rather half-heartedly. In the meantime it had grown quite dark. I looked at his tired little face and said: "Don't you think it's time for bed now? Come along, let's go! Will you come home with me? It's not very far." – "If you want me to." Most of all I wanted to meet the parents of the sad little traveller to Sweden. We were received in a rather unfriendly way; his father with an attitude of duty at all costs, his mother a bundle of anxiety.

"Do you think everything is wonderful in Sweden? We have to work everywhere." – "There are so many forests in Sweden," the boy said in a pensive mood, "and there, people probably don't expect too much of someone as they do here." His large dreamy eyes searched for some moral support, then they wandered anxiously to his father. His father, somewhat shocked by so much unhappy longing in the childlike face, realised for the first time in his life that his own son was an individual with his own desires. He took him in his arms and held him tightly. "Together we'll work out everything and if you tell me all your troubles, I am sure we'll find the way to Sweden."

ca. 520

Malicious Dog For Sale

He was not to blame for his outer appearance. He was a kind of Alsatian with shaggy hair and small, angry eyes. His name was Felix. We were not at all satisfied with him – first of all his barking! He barked every time the telephone rang and kept on barking until the conversation was over. He yelped when the post came. He barked at pedestrians walking past our front window. On top of that, he growled at home: When he had to get off the chair near the radiator, on the counterpane when we wanted to go to bed, he even growled in his sleep, when he dreamed about us. But his barking really caused the trouble; you could even set your watch by it. Felix bit anyone who disturbed him on the sofa after 11 p. m. During the day he bit the postman, the newspaper boy, and errand-boys from the florist's. He even bit short-sighted old ladies who considered him nice enough to stroke, but the worst thing was that he bit every dog in the neighbourhood. No insurance company was prepared to insure him. "The dog has to go!" my wife declared. "The best thing to do is to put a notice in the paper: 'Malicious Dog For Sale, Phone 56991'." – "No one will be interested," my wife said ominously, "who on earth wants to have a malicious dog?" But she was wrong! The next day a gentleman rang up. "Do you have a malicious dog for sale?" – "Yes, that's right!" – "Excuse me, is the dog really malicious?" the gentleman asked. "That cannot be denied. He terrorizes the whole neighbourhood." – "Does he bite?" – "Oh, yes, he bites everyone he comes across. He barks all the time." – "I am not too interested in his barking. I am more concerned whether he bites. How big is he?" – "Oh, about knee-high," I informed him proudly. The gentleman seemed to have made a decision. "I'll take the dog. I am sure we'll agree on the price. Where can I pick him up?" – "54, Green Lane." At that moment we seemed to have been cut off. Anyway, the man did not say anything else. "Hello, are you still there?" I asked. "Oh, yes, yes," he answered hesitatingly, "but unfortunately I cannot take your dog. You did say 54, Green Lane, didn't you?" – "Yes, is anything wrong with our address?" The gentleman seemed to pull himself together and gave an explanation: "Oh no, there is nothing wrong with the address. I live here, too. In fact, I am your next-door neighbour. I was only interested in getting a dog which could give your dog a good beating." The man apologized and put down the receiver. We simply could not sell Felix.

ca. 390

The North

One of the attractions of holidaying in the north of England is the astonishing variety of scenery and things to see and do in such a small area.

There are bustling seaside resorts like Blackpool or Scarborough, the peace of the Cumbrian Pennines, the beauty of the Lake District, the Yorkshire moors and the winding rivers and wooded valleys of the Peak District.

The architectural glories of York Minster and Durham Cathedral and the historical fascination of Hadrian's Wall add to the list of Northern delights, all lying within a few hours' drive of each other.

There is a wide choice, too, when it comes to accommodation – from international standard hotels and friendly guest houses to bed and breakfast in farmhouses and country cottages; and there's plenty of scope for the increasing number of families who prefer the freedom of a self-catering holiday.

Every type of sporting and social activity is available: Plenty of casinos, discos and night clubs in the resorts and towns and rock climbing, sailing and windsurfing for the open-air types.

An important plus about holidaying in the North is the friendly welcome given to visitors. Prices tend to be slightly below those in the south of England, with hotel and guest house owners recognising today's need for value for money.

The most popular destinations are still Blackpool and the Lake District. And the wonderful thing about the Lakes is that no matter how many visitors flock there in high summer it is always possible to find peace and quiet in the hills. That's one of the attractions about the whole of the north – the ease with which one can get off the beaten track. There are plenty of areas where you can drive for miles without seeing another car or sit for hours on a hillside with only the wildlife for company.

The same, of course, applies even more in Scotland, where the choice of holiday is also very wide.

ca. 310

Walking Again

Do it anytime, anywhere, at any pace and for any distance. Whatever your age, walking can help you look and feel fit. Brisk walking burns up about 300 calories an hour and can be an aid controlling weight.
Feet don't cause traffic jams, consume expensive petrol or cause pollution! A brisk walk for just 30 minutes every other day will tone muscles, heart and lungs work more efficiently and work off tension.
What you wear is important. Invest in a good pair of shoes and don't overdress. Heat is a byproduct of exertion and you'll feel quite warm after a few minutes walking. Wear loose clothes that allow arms and legs to move freely.
Don't take a long walk immediately after a meal; wait at least an hour and you'll feel more comfortable and less tired afterwards. Walk briskly and fast enough to breathe deeply and increase your heartbeat rate, but don't overstep your limit. Laboured breathing, pains in the chest or legs and trembling limbs mean it's time to stop. Watch your posture while you're walking. Hold your head up, pull in your stomach and straighten your back. Keep toes pointed straight ahead with your weight resting mainly on the ball of the foot. Start walking now, and you'll be taking steps towards better health. Get off the bus a stop early and tackle the stairs instead of taking the lift. Your feet were made for walking – but make sure they don't get too much of a good thing! Treat them to a footbath at the end of the day to relax aching muscles. After all, if your feet aren't happy, neither are you!

ca. 280

The End Of The World

If Mrs Staffler had been right, you would not be reading this now. She predicted that the world would end in 1969 – and that a few lucky people would be rescued by a fleet of flying saucers!

She urged everyone who wanted to be saved to get to a mountain top near her home in Italy before deadline-day – February 20. That is where the saucers would swoop, looking for survivors, she said.

When not enough people came forward, she arranged for the end of the world to be postponed until March 17.

Nothing special happened on that day either. But shortly afterwards, workmen came to pull down her mountain hut because it had been built without permission!

Lots of other people have also prophesied the end of the world, and have come unstuck. Pilgrims in Devon opted for 1976, and a group of stargazers in Arizona said it would be earlier this year. So when WILL the world end? Old Mother Shipton, a prophetess in Henry VIII's time, predicted 1991.

But scientists estimate that the earth will carry on going round for at least another 70 billion years!

ca. 180

Sanctity Of Life

During the Second World War Raoul Wallenberg saved more than 100,000 Jews from the Nazis. With great courage and personal risk to himself the Swedish diplomat used every trick in the diplomatic bag, and many not even in it, to outwit the Nazi authorities and help save their victims.

Then after the war he was imprisoned by the Russians as a spy. In 1957 the Soviet Union told the Swedish Government that Wallenberg had died 10 years previously in jail.

But reports insist that he is still alive.

Now the British Government has joined an international campaign to press the Russians to co-operate in efforts to discover the facts. The Russians are said to be surprised that so much fuss has been made about the fate of one man.

What a comment on the different attitudes towards human life between the Soviet Union and the West.

ca. 140

Pets

Amid all the excitement of leaving for a new country some people suddenly discover to their horror that a vital member of the family has been overlooked. What, they ask with growing panic, is to be done about the pet dog?

This is a serious matter. For many families, the idea of leaving behind a faithful and perhaps ageing animal is extremely distressing, and the notion of having it put down, unthinkable. In a great many cases, however, there is no need to panic. Animals of all kinds and ages have been successfully transported all over the world. But the rules are complicated and the job must be handled by experts. The largest and oldest established livestock shipping service in the world is run by Spratt's. For more than 100 years, they have been transporting animals of every variety to almost every corner of the globe by land, sea and air.

Their list of past passengers includes chimpanzees, donkeys, fish, hamsters, snakes, squirrels, parrots, and, of course, countless cats and dogs.

ca. 170

New Deal For The Commuters

Plans are afoot next year for the redevelopment of Liverpool Street Station. The scheme, if sanctioned by Parliament, could cause disruption to Eastern **Region** services into London. Work is expected to start on the project soon and will take nine years to complete. When the building is finished it will become one of the biggest stations in Europe.

The multi-million pound complex will incorporate neighbouring Broad Street Station under its roof, which will see the existing station closed down to be replaced by new offices and shops. Sir Robert Lawrence, chairman of the British Rail Board, responsible for co-ordinating the project, said: "The single new station and all the other improvements will give passengers better services and easier interchange facilities with London Transport bus and Underground routes."
A spokesman for British Rail said: "We do expect once work starts on the building that delays will occur. However, ultimately it will mean a better service for all concerned."

ca. 160

Rescued

A widow, who spent 40 hours trapped in her car in last week's blizzards, was rescued only because she decided to feed some birds. As Mrs Greville sat in her car with her dog in a frozen and shocked state, she threw out the remains of the dog's food to the birds, she said yesterday.
The hovering birds attracted the attention of a farmer, who found Mrs Greville stuck in the snow in a remote part of Herefordshire. She was driving home from Sedgley to the little village of Ferryside, when her car broke down. She said: 'It was dark and I couldn't find anyone to help. The blizzard was blowing wildly outside and all I could do was stay in the car and hope. The next day I tried to dig the car out using a biscuit tin lid, but it was impossible. The blizzard was still blowing and I couldn't see anyone to help. As night fell I prepared for a second night in the car. By this time I was bitterly cold and praying for help. The following morning my dog wouldn't eat her food so I threw it out to the birds. A few minutes later the farmer arrived.'

ca. 200

Poison Cloud

A poison gas cloud from a huge chemical fire sent hundreds of people fleeing from homes and schools yesterday.
Dozens were affected by the fumes, from 300 tons of deadly nitrate fertilisers stored in a dockside warehouse near a crowded residential area of Ipswich.
Firemen battling to control the flames faced the additional threat of an explosion. The blaze could be seen seven miles away, and the 750 people evacuated were told not to return home till today.
A full inquiry by the Government's Health and Safety Executive was called for. A fireman said: "I want to know why potentially lethal chemicals were allowed to be stored so close to a densely populated residential area. If the wind had changed and blown the fumes towards the town centre, there could have been a catastrophe." A toxic gas alert also went out at Billingham after a massive blast at a chemical plant. Evacuation plans were drawn up after the explosion, caused by a fractured gas pipe, but gale force winds quickly dispersed the vapour. An investigation is under way.

ca. 190

Schools

Two families who want to send their children to single sex grammar schools are taking their case to the European court. They claim that by forcing the youngsters to attend local comprehensives, the education authority is in breach of the European Convention of Human Rights. Both the children concerned passed examinations for grammar schools but were told that there were not enough places. Instead of going to a Girls' Grammar School, Ann Jones was sent to a comprehensive in her home town of Salisbury. And Mr and Mrs Clark, who had chosen Bishop Wordsworth's Grammar School for their son, found that he had to go to a comprehensive near their home.

Both sets of parents had an appeal to the local education authority rejected on the grounds that there were not enough places at the schools. Last year the intake of each grammar school was cut by 30. At a Press Conference in the House of Lords yesterday, the families claimed that the authority is in breach of Article Two of the Human Rights Convention which guarantees 'every parent the right to have his or her child educated in conformity with his or her religious and philosophical convictions'. If they are successful each of the 104 education authorities would have to provide enough grammar school places for both boys and girls.

ca. 220

Video

Children aged five and six are turning up to school tired after watching films on their parents' home video sets before coming to school in the morning.

Mr L. Ryder, who recently retired as director of Learning Resources at the Inner London Education Authority, said: "We have got this happening in London."

He said that there were millions of video sets in operation in Britain an it had been projected there would be four million by next year.

He added that 38 public libraries were providing video cassettes for hire: "They are not leasing educational programmes – they're leasing programmes which are on the borderline."

A further 64 public libraries were 'actively interested and wanted to develop this service'. The only stipulation was that they were only given to children under 15 if they were accompanied by an adult. "There is an overnight revolution in our homes in terms of the availability of ideas and experience in visual and audio forms," he added. Mr Ryder also added that the Government's plan to give the go ahead to cable television could mean that people in London would receive between 40 and 50 different cables in their homes. "I don't see any debate at all in education about what should be going on cable television directed into the lives of our youngsters, because at the end of it all the impact will have a profound effect on what happens in our classroom. Children will be coming to us with whole new skills and techniques which they may have to 'unlearn' and I am distressed that I see no new groups meeting to discuss what to do. It is no use educationlists being aggressive and argumentative about it. We haven't put forward any view about the way in which this incredible invention of personalized TV should be used and exploited."
Mr Ryder warned that the use of video material would put more stress on the teacher in preparing for lessons but added that using such material would improve the quality of teaching and the effectiveness of what was learned in the classroom.

ca. 350

British Motorists

Britain's City motorists seem to be getting more aggressive, whereas once they were regarded as an example of good manners and politeness. It used to be the Italians honking horn, the Germans speeding and the French cutting in, that were the bane of our motoring lives.

Now the bad behaviour is on our own streets. In recent weeks I have personally experienced so many acts of dangerous driving that I am convinced this is becoming a national disease. Ignoring the appalling behaviour on the motorway where cars travel too close and switch blindly from one lane to another, it is in the cities that the deterioration is most marked.

Because speeds are low and accidents result in only minor damage, the increase in accidents cannot be quantified but one senior police officer told me that the rash of minor accidents was reaching epidemic proportions.

Take my own experience. For four years I ran my last car without receiving a scratch, then I got a new one. Within days a car squeezed past on my inside in a traffic jam and swung left. His rear bumper made a furrow along my nearside wing as he disappeared! On a main road a car approaching from a side street slipped his clutch and rammed my left rear bumper. I got out to inspect the damage and was greeted with a shower of abuse to the effect that I should have given way! In a one-way street I parked – quite legally – and was about to get out when I noticed a car in my rear view mirror. I waited, then heard a loud thump as his nearside door mirror hit my offside rear mirror. He simply roared away as my mirror dropped to the ground.

These minor bumps will cost more than £ 400 – they were the most expensive three weeks in my motoring life.

ca. 300

Aerobics

As of this week, the exercise and keep-fit fans, doing their daily workout in bedrooms, sitting rooms and bathrooms all over Britain, can bob to a different more exciting beat.
The first aerobic exercise tape is now available in Britain, and people have the opportunity to order it at a special low price. Kay Cornelius, one of the most popular teachers at the Aerobic Dance Centre, has now put her Aerobic Workout on tape, with an accompanying booklet to explain the principle of aerobics, and how to do each exercise.
Aerobic exercise is demanding and effective. Its devotees, men as well as women, are not afraid to sweat themselves fit. Their rewards are a trimmer shape, greater strength, increased energy and over-all good health.
Kay Cornelius's workout is a complete fitness programme, which includes three vital elements – toning, stretching and conditioning for the heart and lungs. The basic principles of aerobics were defined by an American heart specialist, who discovered, after a research programme with patients, that exercise which made the heart work harder, could combat heart disease. In order to control your own personal fitness programme, you need to be able to determine – by taking your pulse during exercise – how hard you are making your heart work.
Kay Cornelius gives precise instructions how to do this on her tape, which is designed to provide a programme for beginners as well as a full workout for advanced exercisers.

ca. 230

Riding A Bike

Riding a bike leaves you exposed to injury and even death to a much greater extent than the car driver. Not only can a badly maintained cycle cause accidents you also have to be very cautious of other traffic. It can be difficult to see a cyclist and many motorists seem to suffer from a blind spot where bikes are concerned.
Thousands of cyclists are seriously injured or killed each year and anyone who wants to keep out of the Government statistics must approach the problem from two sides.
The first essential is to make sure the machine you are riding is in the best shape possible. The tyres must be fully inflated and free from damage, the spikes must be tight and you must always have two good brakes. The chain must be tight and the saddle properly adjusted so you can just rest the balls of your feet on the ground. Most adjustments and minor repairs can be made by the rider with the help of a modest tool kit of a couple of spanners, a screwdriver, a pair of pliers and a piece of rag.
Once out on the road clear hand signals are essential but the most important lesson is to look behind before you carry out any manoeuvre. The other drivers may well not be watching you, so you have to watch them. Perhaps the most dangerous manoeuvre is turning right off a main road into a side road. The best procedure is to look back and when the traffic is clear move out from the left-hand side of the road to the outer edge of your lane of traffic. In other words you should stick out your right hand and shift to the middle of the road. Once there you must make it clear by your hand signal that you intend to turn right. Once you are opposite the turn, stop for approaching traffic but still keep signalling. Only when you have plenty of time to get across make your turn so as to end up close to the left-hand curb of the road you have entered.

ca. 350

Remember, Remember: The Fifth Of November

On November Fifth children all over England will go from house to house in small groups. They will take a guy, a figure made of straw, dressed in old clothes or in rags. The children collect money from relatives and acquaintances for fireworks which are let off during the evening.
Boys go about collecting firewood or charcoal for the bonfires. All the material is heaped up for a huge fire in the evening. Those boys who have the largest fire ar very proud.
It is Guy Fawkes Day. In 1605 ten Catholic gentlemen, among them Guy Fawkes of York plotted against King James the First. It is tradition to say that this conspiracy was planned by the Jesuits. The conspirators secretly brought many barrels of gunpowder into the cellars of the Houses of Parliament. On the Fifth of November the King was to open the session of Parliament. Then the conspirators intended to blow up the House, with the King and all his attendants. However, in the night before the opening of Parliament the conspiracy was detected.
Most of the conspirators who had hidden in the cellars of the House, were slain when they tried to flee. The rest, including Guy Fawkes, were taken and executed on the same day.
When night falls on the Fifth of November the bonfires are lit an the fireworks are let off. Finally, Guy Fawkes, the figure of straw, is thrown into the flames and burned to the cheers of the children. Following this, the children stand around the fires and sing or run about with burning sticks. They often repeat their song:
„Remember, remember
the Fifth of November,
gunpowder treason and plot ..."

ca. 280

Education

Black parents are more likely to take an interest in their children's homework than their white counterparts, according to a survey. And trips to the local library can be commonplace among West Indian and Asian families. The new inquiry indicates that black parents' devotion to duty is paying off. It also neatly destroys the theory that black children cannot succeed in the academic race. The survey of 12 Inner London comprehensive schools discloses how white teenagers are often outshone on test day. "When all exam results of both fifth and sixth forms are taken into account, blacks do better than whites," says Professor M. Rutter who headed the fresh probe.
The expert from London University's Institute of Psychiatry points out that many immigrant pupils are merely following their parents. The fact that immigrants arriving in London with few resources buy their own homes within just a few years says an enormous amount for their initiative. True enough. Yet only last month at the British Association for the Advancement of Science Researches claimed racist teachers were turning blacks off school studies. This was the real reason, they said, that so many sporting superstars are black. It was a matter of making a virtue out of necessity. For the fact is that given a good school and a caring home, black children – like whites – can succeed at anything.

ca. 220

Dr Anna Freud

Dr Anna Freud, who died aged 86, was the psychoanalyst daughter of the great pioneer psychoanalyst, Dr Sigmund Freud. With her parents, she settled in London in 1938 after fleeing Nazi persecution of Jews in Vienna. Earlier in the year the Nazis had wanted to interrogate

Sigmund Freud, a sick man of 81, but Anna persuaded them to question her instead. Before she left Vienna she was already chairman of the Vienna Institute of Psychoanalysis. Her father died in 1939 after the outbreak of war.

So after the start of the war she began caring for children who had suffered through it. By 1941 she was running a Hampstead clinic for the treatment of mothers and children emotionally damaged by the war. By 1943 she was operating three rehabilitation nurseries in and around London.

In 1952 she became Director of the Hampstead Child Therapy Course and Clinic. She wrote and edited many books on children and psychoanalysis. A naturalised Briton, she lived on at the Victorian red brick house in Hampstead which was the last home of her father, and which now has a blue plaque outside in his memory. When it was put up in 1956, the proud daughter invited the crowd of her adopted fellow-countrymen standing to watch – "I hope you will all come inside and have a little drink with me."

ca. 220

25 Exciting Years

Life in Britain 25 years ago was almost primitive by today's standards. Fewer than four in ten families owned their own home and central heating was a new idea. Labour-saving devices were the prerogative of the fortunate minority. Compare that with the way we live today. More than half the homes are owned by those who live in them and six in ten have central heating. The housewife's lot is so much easier thanks to new technology and the advent of the affluent society. Then few homes had a freezer and only a third had a fridge or a washing-machine.

Tumble driers and dishwashers were only a gleam in the eye. Now nearly half of us have a freezer. Nearly all homes have a fridge and a washing-machine. Then, shopping was a take-it-or-leave-it drag. There were few self-service stores and even fewer supermarkets. Shop assistants were in short supply and often surly. Now with supermarkets, frozen foods and health foods, shopping has changed radically. And the shopper rules. The revolution in the way we live is revealed in the Consumers' Association magazine "Which?", celebrating its 25th anniversary.

In its jubilee issue, the emphasis is on shopping. Since 1957 the retail price index, the yardstick by which we measure the cost of living, has gone up by more than 560 per cent! So anything which has risen by less than that is now cheaper in real terms than it was 25 years ago.

The number of small grocer's shops will continue to decline and we will not have to worry about shop hours. The things we want to buy will be available seven days a week at all hours.

ca. 290

Health Problems In America

Many Americans spend more time worrying about their health than they do about money. This new finding emerged from a survey of 25,000 men and women along with another piece of news. Women and teenagers feel less healthy than grown men and old couples, who surprisingly, have few complaints. The money-grabbing society has given way to a vast cultural hypochondria and the reason, according to researchers is economic. "People now feel powerless to change their lives," explains one analyst. "They are swept along helplessly on the tide and physical health is their last bastion of personal control. Here is something they can influence."

Money problems now concern 42 per cent of those surveyed less than the state of their own bodies, which they think about constantly. They run, diet, and force themselves to adhere to monastic regimes in their search for the Holy Grail of health. The average person questioned exercises six hours a week and one in four works out for over an hour a day. But then as one professor points out, "Americans are obsessed with excess. Moderation is not a popular concept." And out of this national characteristic has developed what is known as 'sick chic'. While it is unfashionable to be really ill, which just proves you have not been eating your wholegrain bread and running four miles a day, it is smart to have certain ailments.

ca. 230

Does Your Dog Need A Diet Too?

If I can believe even half of what I read in the papers nearly everybody is interested in diet and the effects it has on health. Their own diet that is! And their own health. Far fewer pay much attention to the diet and health of their dogs. The result is not that dogs are starving. Quite the reverse. Maybe as many as one British dog in three is much too fat! Even more disturbing is the fact that fat people are most likely to own fat dogs. Statistics are difficult to come by, but some years ago an animal hospital attempted it. They found that from a sample thousand, only 35 could be classified as thin, and a massive 277 were seriously overweight. Even so, only three had been taken to the hospital because of obesity. The others had gone along to have their nails trimmed, to be treated for bad breath or breathlessness. And one because, when not eating, it merely slept. As with humans, so with dogs, fatness kills. Not

directly, but through the conditions, principally heart disease, encouraged by obesity. Moreover fat dogs lose all interest in life and only enjoy eating!
And there's a simple, do-it-yourself way of diagnosing your pet's condition, for which you need only an unprejudiced mind, a good eye and sensitive fingertips. Dogs whose bones show clearly through their skin are thin. If not excessive, this is nothing to worry about. Those with ribs you can just see or feel with fingertips are normal. Those whose rib cage is not discernible, and under whose skin you can feel a layer of fat, are obese, and therefore at risk.

ca. 270

Facts About The Freeze

The month of January will probably be remembered for its blizzards and the chaos which came with them. There is no doubt that the snowfall which began at the beginning of January has few equals for its intensity – incredible that so much snow could have fallen within 48 hours, according to a weather report written by Mr J. Powell, who keeps the records from weather stations. The snow stopped on a Saturday morning but a strong easterly gale whipped up clouds of the fine powdery snow for a further two days, clogging up the roads of the area, bringing traffic to a standstill, and forcing many people to walk. The bitterly cold weather continued for nine days, and there were innumerable burst pipes with the temperature remaining below freezing day and night. The queues for bread and milk brought back vivid memories for the older generation. The temperatures in the valleys could have been much lower, since the heavier cold air often slides down the mountainsides, but one of the weather stations measured no low records.

The coldest day was January 10 with a temperature of −7,4 centigrade. And the warmest day was January 3 with a temperature of 8,1 centigrade. The thaw set in with the return of persistent hill fog on January 15 and most of the snow disappeared, although a few patches remained until the end of the month. Total rainfall during the month measured 7,7 inches and on the wettest day 1,2 inches of rain fell. There were five days of snow, seven sunny days, 10 'dry' days, 15 days of fog and 18 days of rain. Surprisingly the month was not nearly as cold as the previous January and even warmer than December. The month was slightly wetter than usual.

ca. 290

A Winebook

Wine is one of Britain's fastest growing industries. Consumption has trebled in the last 10 years, and now all kinds of people have jumped on the bandwagon, while a lot of rubbish is written about it.
'The Wine Drinker's Handbook', however, is the best book on the subject I have seen for a long time. In it, Serena Sutcliffe, who is a Master of Wine, speaks plainly and almost literally about the subject. The book, enjoyable to read and full of practical, straightforward and accurate information, is published in hardback.
The delicatessen business is also booming – to the tune of a staggering £ 562 million a year. Glynn Christian, broadcaster on good eating and good cooking, used to work behind the counter in his own delicatessen. His 'Delicatessen Food Handbook' is absolutely splendid: A book full of invaluable details about vinegar, truffles, yoghurt, snails, pickles, tea, oil, herbs and spices. Did you know, for instance, that a thin slice of black olive is almost indistinguishable as a garnish from a slice of truffle? Or that gin and pineapple have an astonishing affinity which is very appealing when hot?

ca. 190

Radiation

Householders are to take part in a two-year survey to see how much natural radiation they are exposed to in their own homes. A study in Devon and Cornwall has already shown that people who live in areas where there is plenty of granite are exposed to a greater amount of radiation.

More than 2,000 British homes will take part in the survey. It involves placing technical devices in their bedrooms and living rooms, to find out the amount of radiation they get from gamma rays and the radioactive gas radon.

The survey also claims to discover how the amount of radiation varies with the type of building materials, the location, and the amount of insulation. Scientists already know from work in the late 1950 that people in Aberdeen – where granite is common – are exposed to 50 per cent more gamma rays than people in Edinburgh where sandstone dominates.

These rays are similar to X-rays, and probably account for 16 per cent of people's exposure to radiation from all sources. They are emitted from radioactive substances in building materials and the ground.

Radon gas is formed naturally in rocks, soil and building materials, and seeps indoors. When inhaled, radon and the products of its radioactive decay give a radiation dose to the lungs.

ca. 210

Die "TOP 15" aus dem C. Bange Verlag

Klaus Sczyrba
Das neue große Aufsatzbuch
- Methoden und Beispiele des Aufsatzunterrichts für die Sekundarstufe I und II - Alles zur Technik des Aufsatzschreibens, Stoffsammlung und Disposition.
213 Seiten - 6. erw. Auflage
Best. Nr. 0698-X

Klaus Sczyrba
Wege zum guten Aufsatz
Übungsbuch für das 3. bis 5. Schuljahr
Alle Aufsatzarten und Aufgaben zu Wortwahl, Satzbau und Grammatik mit angegl. Lösungsteil.
162 Seiten - viele Illustr.
Best. Nr. 0690-4

Egon Ecker
Wie interpretiere ich Gedichte?
Hilfen und Anleitungen zum Interpretieren von Gedichten.
168 Seiten
Best. Nr. 0695-5

Martin H. Ludwig
Praktische Rhetorik
Reden - Argumentieren - Erfolgreich verhandeln - Grafiken - Anleitungen für Schule und Beruf!
162 Seiten - 3. Auflage -
Best. Nr. 0688-2

Albert Lehmann
Erörterungen
Gliederungen und Materialien - Methoden und Beispiele.
DAS Buch in Sachen Erörterungen!!
184 Seiten - 6. überarbeitete Auflage März 94
Best. Nr. 0490-1

Edgar Neis
Wie interpretiere ich ein Drama
Dramatische Formen - Methode des Interpretierens - Wege zur Erschließung und Analyse.
4. überarb. Auflage -
236 Seiten
Best. Nr. 0697-1

Edgar Neis
Wie interpretiere ich Gedichte und Kurzgeschichten
Ein "Grundkurs", die Kunst des Interpretierens zu erlernen und zu verstehen.
15. Auflage - 208 Seiten -
Best. Nr. 0584-3

Methoden und Beispiele der Kurzgeschichteninterpretation
Information und Nachschlagewerk für den Unterricht in den Sekundarstufen.
4. Auflage - 114 Seiten -
Best. Nr. 0691-2

Klaus Sczyrba
Lebensnahe Grammatik für die Grundschule
Das grammatische Handwerkszeug für Schüler, Eltern und Lehrer.
2. Auflage - 140 Seiten -
Best. Nr. 0673-4

Klaus Sczyrba
Lebensnahe Grammatik für die Sekundarstufe I
Anhand von 100 Übungen und Lösungen werden hier alle grammatikalisch wichtigen Regeln aufgezeigt.
3. Auflage - 128 Seiten -
Best. Nr. 0474-X

Klaus Sczyrba
Lebensnahe Diktate für das 2. bis 4. Schuljahr
Mit 150 Diktaten hilft das Buch die Rechtschreibleistungen der Grundschüler zu verbessern.
5. Auflage - 152 Seiten + Lösungsteil
Best. Nr. 0610-6

Klaus Sczyrba
Lebensnahe Diktate für das 5. bis 10. Schuljahr
250 Diktate, Übungsmöglichkeiten und Tabellen der Rechtschreibschwierigkeiten machen dieses Buch unerlässlich für Lehrer, Schüler und Eltern.
4. Auflage - 432 Seiten
Best. Nr. 0612-2

Klaus Sczyrba
Komm, wir schreiben!
Rechtschreibübungsheft für das **2. und 3. Schuljahr**
3. Auflage - DIN A4 -
Best. Nr. 0614-9

Komm, wir schreiben!
Rechtschreibübungsheft für das **3. und 4. Schuljahr**
3. überarb. Auflage - DIN A4 -
Best. Nr. 0699-8

Komm, wir schreiben!
Rechtschreibübungsheft für das **4. und 5. Schuljahr**
Neuerscheinung - DIN A4 -
Best. Nr. 0479-0

Alle mit 4-farbigem Umschlag und zweifarbigem Innenteil!

Unsere Anschrift:

C. Bange Verlag GmbH & Co. KG
Marienplatz 12   96142 Hollfeld
Postfach 1160   96139 Hollfeld

Telefon: 0 92 74 / 3 72
Telefax: 0 92 74 / 8 02 30